Stories of
Mermaids

Russell Punter

Illustrated by
Desideria Guicciardini

Reading Consultant: Alison Kelly
Roehampton University

Contents

Chapter 1

The ghostly galleon

Harmony lived with her
mother at the very bottom
of the ocean.

They were so poor they could only afford a tiny cave. This was cramped, dark and very cold. It froze their fins and took the shine off their scales.

Harmony tried to keep up their spirits by singing beautiful songs. Her voice was so enchanting that passing fish had to stop and listen.

One day, Harmony's mother woke up shivering all over. She was covered in blue spots and her tongue had turned purple.

Harmony rushed to find Dr. Finley.

Say ahh.

"Your mother is very sick,"
he whispered to Harmony,
"The only cure is polkadot
seaweed, taken twice a day for
one week."

"Where can I find that?"
asked Harmony.

"That's the problem," replied
Dr. Finley. "It only grows in
the Pirates' Graveyard."

"Oh no," gasped Harmony. "Not that spooky place full of sunken pirate ships?"

"I'm afraid so," replied the doctor.

"They say it's haunted by the ghost of Gingerbeard," said Harmony with a shiver. "He was the fiercest pirate to sail the Seven Seas."

The thought of visiting the graveyard filled Harmony with fear, but she had no choice. Minutes later, she was swimming nervously between the creepy wrecks.

Harmony searched countless ships without luck. She had almost given up hope, when she saw something spotty sticking out of a rusty old cannon.

Found it!

Suddenly, a terrifying figure appeared from nowhere.

Yahahahaha!

Harmony yelped in fright. It was Gingerbeard's ghost.

"Come to steal my treasure, eh?" snarled the pirate.

"No," cried Harmony. "I just need the polkadot weed to cure my mother."

A likely story, fish features.

"I don't believe you," cackled Gingerbeard. He grabbed Harmony roughly and locked her in a cabin.

"No one gets their hands on my gold," screamed the ghost. With that, he shimmered off to patrol the top deck.

What will happen to my mother now?

Harmony felt terrible. She tried to cheer herself up by singing, but all her songs came out sounding sad.

12

Harmony's lovely voice
floated around Gingerbeard's
ship. No matter where he went,
the pirate could hear her.

However hard he tried,
Gingerbeard couldn't drag
himself away from the
mermaid's tragic tunes.

As each day passed, he began
to feel as sorry for Harmony as
a tough old pirate can.

After a week of the singing,
Gingerbeard had had enough.
"I can't take any more!" he
sobbed. "Please just go home
and take this chest with you."

Harmony swam home as fast as she could and opened the chest.

Polkadot weed floated out, along with handfuls of coins.

Harmony's mother was cured and, thanks to Gingerbeard's gold, they moved into a warm and cosy new cave.

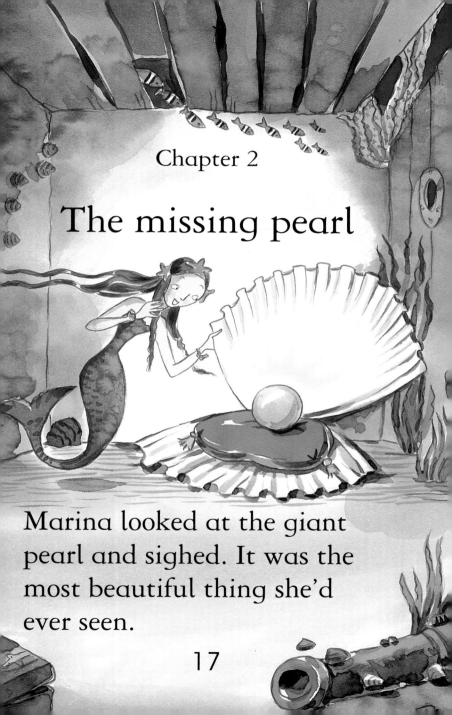

Chapter 2

The missing pearl

Marina looked at the giant
pearl and sighed. It was the
most beautiful thing she'd
ever seen.

17

According to legend, anyone who owned the pearl would never grow old and could swim the oceans forever. Sharks guarded it day and night.

Okay, Toothy – time to lock up.

Right-o, Razor.

Giant Pink Pearl

VIEWINGS DAILY
9am - 5pm

The magical pearl was first prize in King Neptune's Great Seahorse Race.

The event was part of the king's one-hundreth birthday celebrations. Marina was sure that she and her seahorse Swish could win.

SWISH

Marina had been preparing for months with Scuba, her trainer.

"Make sure Swish has an early night," she told him.

As Marina swam off, a sneaky-looking pair peeked out from behind a rock.

"Our slowcoach of a seahorse won't stand a chance against Swish," whispered Sid the squid. "And Marina is the ocean's best rider."

20

The mermaid by his side flicked her tail and gave a wicked smile. "We'll see about that," she said.

Just wait.

"What are you going to do, Storm?" asked Sid.

"I have a plan that can't fail," she replied. "That pearl is as good as ours."

21

Next morning, the seahorses and their riders lined up for the big race.

Marina gently stroked Swish's neck. "You can do it, boy," she whispered.

Storm looked across smugly
at Marina. Then she turned
and winked at her trainer.

Sid winked back and swam
away.

What are those
two up to?

As Marina passed the reef, a cloud of thick, black ink shot out in front of her. Quick as a flash, Swish leapt over the top.

Marina lost hold of the reins as Swish sailed over the ink cloud. The others, spotting the hazard ahead, swerved quickly past.

"Lucky you're such a good jumper, Swish," said Marina as she took the reins again.

As they raced off, she just spotted an inky tentacle dart back into the coral.

They soon caught up, and were neck and neck with Storm as the finish line came in sight.

With a final burst, Swish sped forward to win.

Everyone clustered around to congratulate Marina. Everyone except Storm, that is. She was busy whispering something to Sid, who slithered off quickly.

Three cheers for the winner!

A few minutes later, they were all in the cabin of the old shipwreck for the prize-giving ceremony.

But they were in for a shock. The pearl had gone.

The shark guards searched everywhere, but the pearl was nowhere to be seen.

"It must have been stolen!" cried Scuba.

"But how?" asked Toothy, the guard. "This room was locked."

The second guard pointed to a tiny porthole. "That's the only other way in and out."

"But it's too small to get the pearl through," said Sid.

"Then it must have been taken before we locked up," said Toothy.

"Who was the last one alone with the pearl?" asked Storm, with a glint in her eye.

Toothy pointed a fin at Marina.

I'm innocent!

"She only took part in the race so we wouldn't suspect her," sneered Storm.

"Yeah," added Sid, waving his tentacles. "She only won by chance."

Marina desperately tried to think of a way to prove her innocence. Suddenly, Sid's dirty tentacles gave her an idea.

"I think the pearl is still in this room!" she cried, pointing at a pile of old cannonballs. She frantically rubbed each one with her seaweed necklace.

"Look! This one isn't a cannonball at all," she declared.

"The pearl!" gasped the crowd.

"Covered in squid ink!" added Marina, staring at Sid.

Gulp!

"She made me do it!" cried Sid, pointing at Storm. "I had to disguise the pearl so Storm could collect it later."

"Shush, you stupid squid!" yelled Storm. But it was too late. The two crooks were led away and Marina was presented with her magical pearly prize.

Chapter 3

The dancing mermaid

Coral loved living under the sea. She raced dolphins and sealions.

35

She swam
with schools
of shimmering
sardines...

she teased
sharks...

Z Z Z Z

and spent
the summer
splashing in
the surf.

But Coral had a secret wish.
She wanted to dance.

Every evening, she watched
the humans whirling and
spinning at the dance hall.
She longed to join in.

37

Coral looked down sadly at her tail. "How can I dance without legs?" she sighed. "I'd give anything to change my flippers for feet."

As she swam past Neptune's palace, Coral had an idea. "Perhaps the king can help me!" With a thrust of her tail, she darted inside.

Coral entered the throne room nervously. Her tummy felt as if it was full of butterfly fish.

"And what can I do for you, young lady?" boomed the king.

"W...well your majesty," Coral began, "I'd like some legs please."

"Legs?" repeated the puzzled king. "Mermaids don't need legs."

Coral told the king about her secret wish. At first, he looked doubtful, but Coral begged and begged.

"I will grant your wish for one week," he said. "Then you must decide whether to keep your legs or your tail."

Coral wanted to dance more than anything, so she agreed.

King Neptune pointed his magical trident at Coral's tail. A sparkling swirl shot out...

and the next thing she knew, Coral was *standing* on the beach.

She tried to run to the dance hall. But her new legs took some getting used to...

After a lot of practice, Coral walked into the hall. The crowd began to whisper. Who was the beautiful stranger with silky, golden hair?

Soon she was swept off her new feet by a handsome young fisherman called Dan.

They spent all night gliding and whirling around the floor.

Coral had never been so happy. But she soon found that life on land wasn't as good as it looked.

43

Walking was a lot more tiring than swimming...

fish weren't so much fun when they were stuck in a bowl...

and Coral's tail had never felt as sore as her feet.

Dancing with Dan was the only thing that made it worthwhile.

44

Coral told Dan her amazing secret. A week later, they went to the rocks to meet the king.

Neptune rose from the waves. "So, what is your decision?" he asked Coral. "Legs or tail?"

Coral had missed her ocean home more than she had enjoyed dancing. But she had fallen in love with Dan.

"Legs," she murmured faintly.

The king looked at Dan. "And which do *you* think she should choose?" he asked.

Dan was in love with Coral, but he'd seen how sad she was on land. "Tail," he said.

Coral was heartbroken by his reply. But the king smiled wisely and whispered another question in the fisherman's ear. Dan grinned and nodded.

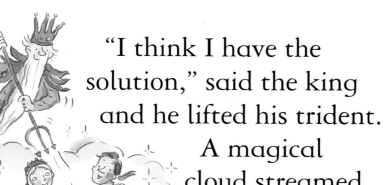

"I think I have the
solution," said the king
and he lifted his trident.
A magical
cloud streamed
around the pair.

The next second, Coral was
back in the sea. She had a tail
instead of legs – and so did Dan!
"Let's try underwater
dancing," said Coral. And they
swam off, hand-in-hand.

47

Series editor:
Lesley Sims

This edition first published in 2007 by Usborne Publishing Ltd.,
Usborne House, 83-85 Saffron Hill, London EC1N 8RT, England.
www.usborne.com
Copyright © 2007, 2005 Usborne Publishing Ltd.